DATE DUE

SE 2 5 '99			
FE 3 '00			
MR 24 '00			
MY 19 '00			
DE 4 '00			
MR 2 7 '01			

Canopy Crossing

A Story of an Atlantic Rainforest

The Nature Conservancy®

To Asha, who wrote all her term papers
about the rainforest. — A.N.

To Lin. — T.B.

Book copyright © 1997 Trudy Corporation, 353 Main Avenue, Norwalk, CT 06851.

Soundprints is a division of Trudy Corporation, Norwalk, Connecticut.

Book Design: Shields & Partners, Westport, CT

First Edition 1997
10 9 8 7 6 5 4 3 2 1
Printed in Hong Kong

Acknowledgements:
    Our very special thanks to Dr. James M. Dietz of the University of Maryland's Department of Zoology for his review and guidance.
    The illustrator would like to thank Ann for her invaluable help in providing reference for the illustrations.

Library of Congress Cataloging-in-Publication Data

Nagda, Ann Whitehead, 1945-

Canopy crossing : a story of an Atlantic rainforest / by Ann Whitehead Nagda ; illustrated by Thomas Buchs.
        p.   cm.
Summary: Describes some of the plants and other animals that a black-faced lion tamarin encounters in the Atlantic rainforest of Brazil as he searches for a mate to start a family of his own.
        ISBN 1-56899-449-4 (hardcover)   ISBN 1-56899-450-8 (pbk.)
1. Leontopithecus chrysopygus — Juvenile literature.
2. Rainforest animals — Juvenile literature[1. Tamarins. 2. Monkeys.
3. Rainforest animals.]   I. Buchs, Thomas, ill. II. Title.
        QL737.P92N33 1997   96-39091
        599. 8'4 — dc21   CIP
                                                                          AC

Canopy Crossing

A Story of an Atlantic Rainforest

by Ann Whitehead Nagda
Illustrated by Thomas Buchs

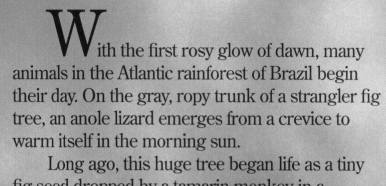

W ith the first rosy glow of dawn, many animals in the Atlantic rainforest of Brazil begin their day. On the gray, ropy trunk of a strangler fig tree, an anole lizard emerges from a crevice to warm itself in the morning sun.

Long ago, this huge tree began life as a tiny fig seed dropped by a tamarin monkey in a mahogany tree. The seed landed on decaying leaves in a tree fork and started to grow. Roots from the fig plant hugged the tree as they descended to the forest floor. Eventually these roots strangled and killed the mahogany tree and it rotted away.

Now, the hollow trunk of the strangler fig is filled with early morning activity.

Nearby, a black-faced lion tamarin snoozes in a tree-hole in a large tapia tree. An hour after dawn, the small monkey awakens. He peers from the hole, making sure no enemies are lurking outside. As he slips out of his den, he grips the trunk with his claws and scrambles upward.

Heavy rain has fallen during the night. Everything is wet — the leaves, the bark, the branches. Water droplets on a spider web catch the light and shimmer like pearls. The tamarin sniffs the air and smells damp wood and decaying leaves. Thirsty after a long night's sleep, he laps water from a leaf.

The tamarin stops to look around again — he is not safe when he is alone. Several weeks ago, he left his family group to start his own family, but he has had no luck. He whines and clucks to see if other tamarins are in the area. No one answers his call.

He jumps to the branches
of a strangler fig tree and squeezes
a green fig, hoping for a bite to eat. But it
has not developed into a ripe red fruit yet. He
watches as a wasp burrows into a fig to lay her
eggs. Pollen clinging to her body will dust the
miniature flowers inside. In a few weeks, tiny
wasps will hatch from her eggs and fly away to
pollinate other fig trees. Because the mother wasp
has brought pollen, the fig will develop seeds and
turn into a tasty, ripe fruit.

Spotting the anole lizard sunning itself on the trunk, the tamarin springs after it. The lizard runs around the trunk and disappears. The tamarin reaches inside several small crevices, but cannot find the lizard.

He glances around for something else to eat. Above the treetops that form the rainforest canopy, he sees movement. He freezes in terror as a harpy eagle dives toward him, its talons sharp and menacing.

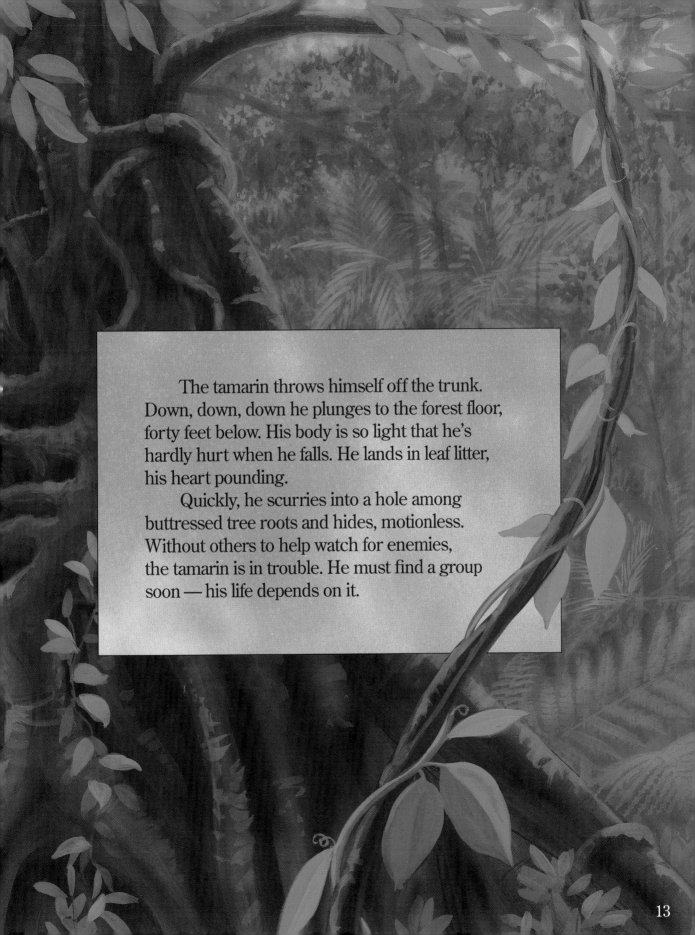

The tamarin throws himself off the trunk.
Down, down, down he plunges to the forest floor,
forty feet below. His body is so light that he's
hardly hurt when he falls. He lands in leaf litter,
his heart pounding.

Quickly, he scurries into a hole among
buttressed tree roots and hides, motionless.
Without others to help watch for enemies,
the tamarin is in trouble. He must find a group
soon — his life depends on it.

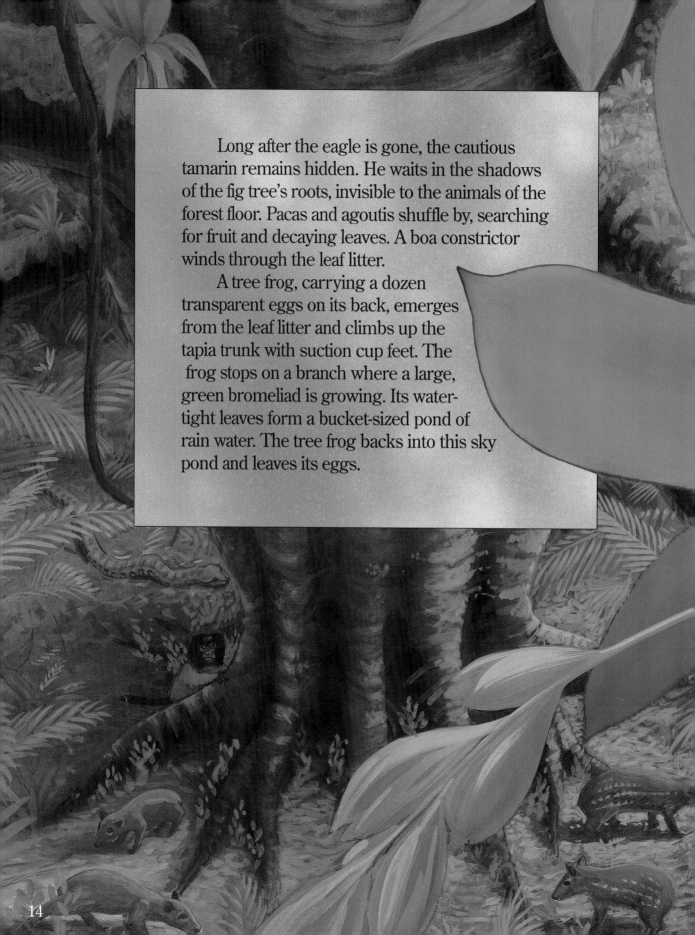

Long after the eagle is gone, the cautious tamarin remains hidden. He waits in the shadows of the fig tree's roots, invisible to the animals of the forest floor. Pacas and agoutis shuffle by, searching for fruit and decaying leaves. A boa constrictor winds through the leaf litter.

A tree frog, carrying a dozen transparent eggs on its back, emerges from the leaf litter and climbs up the tapia trunk with suction cup feet. The frog stops on a branch where a large, green bromeliad is growing. Its water-tight leaves form a bucket-sized pond of rain water. The tree frog backs into this sky pond and leaves its eggs.

The sun is high when the tamarin leaves his hiding place and looks around nervously. He climbs to the bromeliad, frightening an azure jay away from the pond. Using his long, thin fingers, the hungry tamarin probes between the leaves that form the pond. He pulls out a green katydid and eats it, head first. Then he snatches a small lizard. From the bromeliad's crimson-red blossom, a hermit hummingbird drinks nectar.

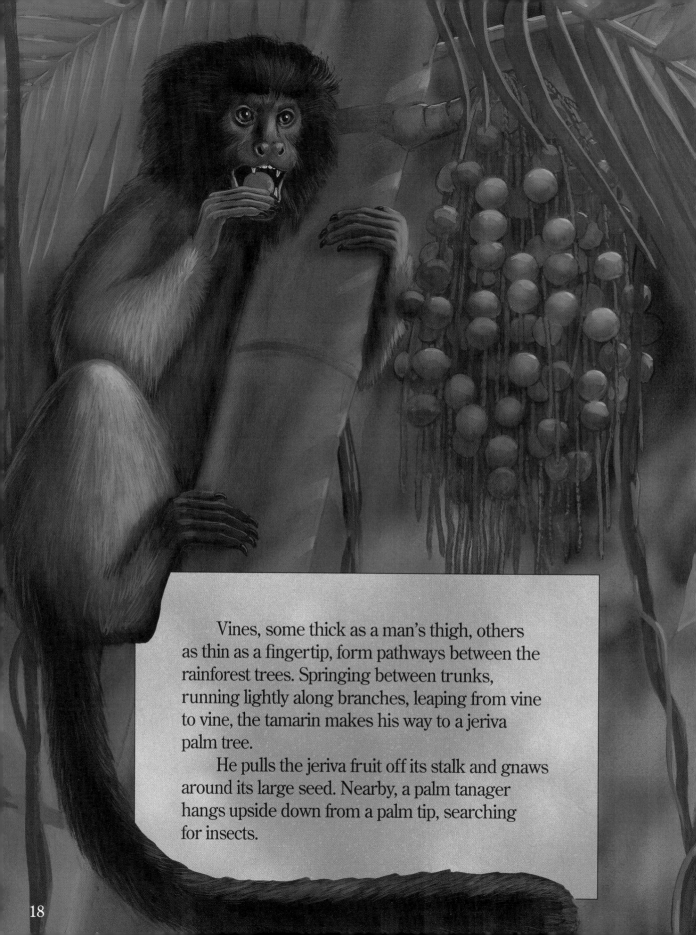

Vines, some thick as a man's thigh, others as thin as a fingertip, form pathways between the rainforest trees. Springing between trunks, running lightly along branches, leaping from vine to vine, the tamarin makes his way to a jeriva palm tree.

He pulls the jeriva fruit off its stalk and gnaws around its large seed. Nearby, a palm tanager hangs upside down from a palm tip, searching for insects.

The tamarin hears rustling leaves and sees flashes of gold fur. With chattering clucks, a group of lion tamarins arrives to feed on the palm fruit. The tamarin tenses as a strange male walks toward him stiff-legged. Hairs on both male's manes stand up straight, making their heads look bigger. The strange male chatters angrily, then jumps on the tamarin, biting and scratching him. The tamarin leaps away. This group will not accept him — they already have enough adult males.

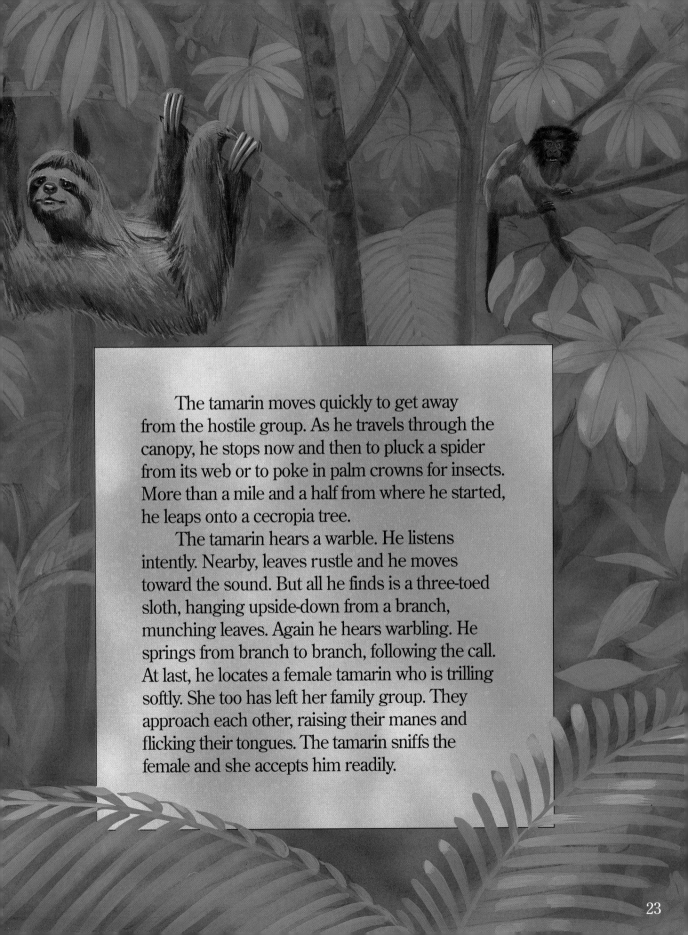

The tamarin moves quickly to get away from the hostile group. As he travels through the canopy, he stops now and then to pluck a spider from its web or to poke in palm crowns for insects. More than a mile and a half from where he started, he leaps onto a cecropia tree.

The tamarin hears a warble. He listens intently. Nearby, leaves rustle and he moves toward the sound. But all he finds is a three-toed sloth, hanging upside-down from a branch, munching leaves. Again he hears warbling. He springs from branch to branch, following the call. At last, he locates a female tamarin who is trilling softly. She too has left her family group. They approach each other, raising their manes and flicking their tongues. The tamarin sniffs the female and she accepts him readily.

The female tamarin follows him to a tree full of ripe figs, and together they feast on the sweet fruit. They are messy eaters. Pieces of fruit drop to the forest floor where agoutis and pacas feed on them. White-lipped peccaries are also drawn to the rain of fruit. A flock of red-tailed parrots lands in the tree and pecks at the figs, too.

When the tamarins finish eating, they spring through the canopy together. With their stomachs full of fruit, they soon spread tiny fig seeds in their droppings. Some of the seeds will sprout and new strangler fig trees will grow, providing homes and food for many rainforest creatures.

The two tamarins will stay together and someday they will raise a family of their own. They spend the rest of the day hunting for fruit and insects. They take turns watching for enemies, safer now because they have each other. When the sun begins to set and the forest darkens, they locate a tree hole and climb inside. Snuggling close, they keep each other warm until morning.

Guaraqueçaba, Brazil

Black-faced lion tamarins are found only in Guaraqueçaba, a 775,000 acre
wildlife protection area in Brazil that contains the largest remaining area
of Atlantic rainforest. More than half of the world's remaining tropical
rainforest is in Central and South America.

About the Atlantic Rainforest

B efore the Portuguese explorers discovered Brazil in the early 1500s, a great forest extended from the northern tip of Brazil 1500 miles south into Paraguay. This great forest is called Atlantic rainforest, because it receives more than one hundred inches of rain a year. Today, only eight percent of the Atlantic rainforest remains. The rest was destroyed to make way for coffee and cocoa plantations, rubber trees, cattle pasture, and logging. This story takes place in Guaraqueçaba (pronounced Gwar-uh-kay-saba) a 775,000 acre wildlife protection area in Brazil that contains the largest remaining area of Atlantic rainforest. After the park was created in 1989, black-faced lion tamarins were discovered there.

There are four kinds of lion tamarin monkeys that live only in the Atlantic rainforest — the golden, black, golden-headed, and black-faced lion tamarin. These different kinds of tamarin look very similar, with long tails and lion-like manes, and are about the size of a squirrel. Lion tamarins usually live in groups of two to eleven. Each tamarin in the group helps to look for danger as the group moves through the forest looking for food. Tamarins help each other with child care, too. Lion tamarins normally give birth to twins. Carrying two babies takes a lot of energy, so the father or older brothers and sisters carry and care for the babies — the mother tamarin needs her strength to produce milk.

The lion tamarins need two things in their environment — tree-holes for sleeping and bromeliads (pronounced bro-mill-ee-adds) for food and water. Both of these can be found in primary uncut forests — forests that have not been cut down and regrown — and there aren't many of those left. All of the lion tamarins are in great danger of disappearing. Diseases, capture by humans, and a habitat that is getting smaller have all reduced the number of tamarins that live in the wild. Scientists estimate that less than 300 black-faced lion tamarins remain.

Glossary

 *Agouti*

 *Cecropia Leaves*

 *Katydid*

 *Anole Lizard*

 *Harpy Eagle*

 *Tapia Tree*

 *Azteca Ants on Cecropia Tree*

 *Hermit Humming-bird*

 *Three-toed Sloth*

 *Azure Jays*

 *Jeriva Palm Fruit*

 *White-lipped Peccaries*

 *Cecropia Fruits*

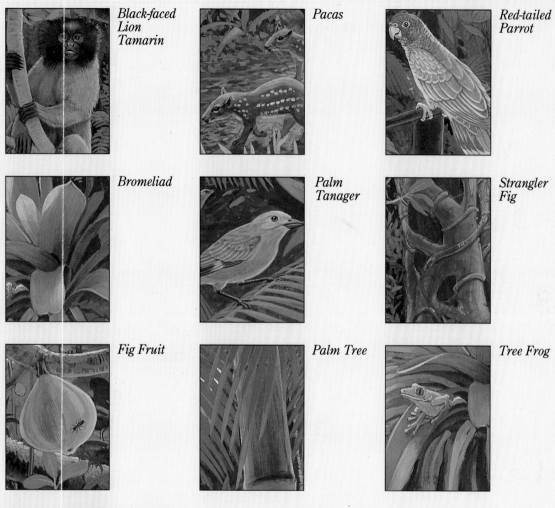

Black-faced
Lion
Tamarin

Pacas

Red-tailed
Parrot

Bromeliad

Palm
Tanager

Strangler
Fig

Fig Fruit

Palm Tree

Tree Frog

Fig Wasp